MW00885115

# 2nd Opportunity Program Personal Re-entry Plan

AUGIE GHILARDUCCI

This plan belongs to:

_____

Copyright © 2022 Augie Ghilarducci

All rights reserved. No part of this packet may be reproduced or used in any manner without the written permission of the copyright owner.

ISBN: 9798872375036

# CONTENTS

A Path Forward©                          1

A Path to Financial Freedom©             9

Values-Aligned Goal Setting©            15

A Path to Advanced Skills©              31

A Path to Higher Education©             35

Resume Worksheet                        37

Re-entry Checklist                      39

About the Author                        41

# INTRODUCTION

This personal re-entry plan was designed to accompany the 2nd Opportunity Program. The program was created and is presented by those with the lived experience of incarceration. The information, stories, and experiences are based upon the successful re-entry of our thought leadership team, with more than 100 years of combined incarceration.

The questions and activities in this packet are designed to help you organize your thoughts for your next steps, whether it be continuing your sentence or reintegrating into society. Completing this plan requires effort, as your private work is grounded in your thoughts, situation, opportunities, and challenges. It provides you with a way to use the material we present and customize it to your situation. Feel free to use as much paper as necessary to fully organize your thoughts.

Not everything in this program will necessarily have immediate meaning to you, or perhaps ever. However, I assure you there is something in this for everyone who is presently incarcerated. It is something you will want to refer to, update from time to time, and bring with you when you walk out the door.

The program is designed to have you watch videos that discuss many topics important to successful re-entry. There are questions and activities in this packet for every video. While it's probably better to do them at the time you complete the video, it is not necessary. Do what works best for you. You can always complete them later or not at all. This is not a punishment; it is something to show you that there are great things you can do after this is over.

We welcome you and your family to contact us at 2ndopp.com or email reentry@2ndopp.com. We wish you the very best, and please know there is an opportunity to rebuild your life on the other side. We are here to help in that process.

# A PATH FORWARD©

## Video 1 – Introduction

What do you imagine your future will look like after your release from incarceration?

_____
_____
_____
_____
_____
_____
_____

## Video 2 – Section 1. Trauma

What traumatic events in your life have shaped the way you see the world?

_____
_____
_____
_____
_____
_____
_____

## Video 3 – Section 2. Posttraumatic Growth

What things can you point to where you demonstrated your ability to overcome a bad situation?

_____
_____
_____
_____
_____
_____
_____

## Video 4 – Section 3. A Parallel Path

Explore the U.S. Department of Labor website MyNextMove.org for information and assistance about finding the right career based on activities you enjoy. **MyNextMove.org** is an extremely valuable tool for career planning that allows you to create an account and includes average salaries, demand forecasts for various occupations, and pathways for advancement within a career.

Whether or not you have the skills or education today, write down some careers that you might want to pursue.

_____

_____
_____
_____
_____
_____
_____
_____
_____

## Video 5 – Section 4. Setting Career Goals

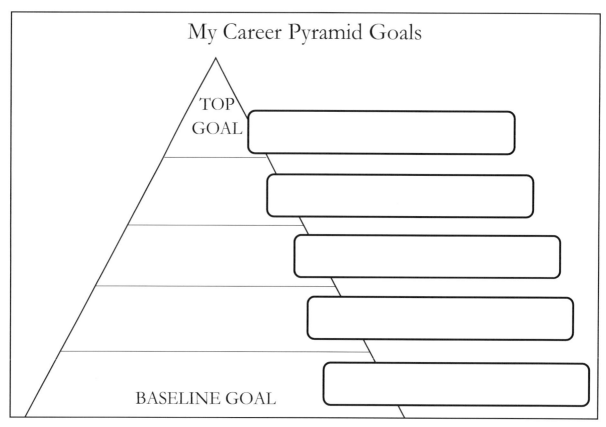

Start by entering your Top Goal (your ultimate career), then go to the Baseline Goal and fill in each step to get to the Top Goal. Please refer to the video for an explanation and example.

## Video 6 – Section 5. Developing a Resume

Please take the time to prepare a written list and explanation of your skills for a potential employer.

_____
_____
_____
_____
_____
_____

### Video 7 – Section 6. Communication Skills

What can you do to improve your communications skills in your current environment?

_____

_____

_____

_____

_____

_____

_____

### Video 8 – Section 7. Crafting Your Story

Write out your elevator pitch.

_____

_____

_____

_____

_____

_____

_____

_____

_____

_____

_____

_____

_____

### Video 9 – Section 8. The Job Interview

1.  **Can you tell me a little about yourself?** Give a concise, compelling pitch that shows exactly why you are the right person for the job.

_____

_____

_____

_____

_____

_____

_____

2.  **Why do you want this job?** Identify a few key factors that make the role a great fit for you.

_____

_____

_____
_____
_____
_____
_____

3.  **Why should we hire you?** A) that you can do the work and deliver great results; B) that you'll fit in with the team and culture; C) that you'd be a better hire than any of the other candidates.

_____
_____
_____
_____
_____
_____
_____

4.  **What are your greatest professional strengths?** Share your strengths and follow up with an example of how you've demonstrated these traits in your life.

_____
_____
_____
_____
_____
_____

5.  **What do you consider to be your weaknesses?** Think of something that you struggle with but are working to improve.

_____
_____
_____
_____
_____
_____

6.  **What is your greatest professional achievement?** Spend the bulk of your time describing what you did (the action) and what you achieved (the result).

_____
_____
_____
_____
_____
_____

7. **Where do you see yourself in five years?** Be honest and specific about your future goals.

_____

_____

_____

_____

_____

_____

8. **What are you looking for in a new position?** Be specific and point out some of the things the position you are applying for has to offer.

_____

_____

_____

_____

_____

_____

9. **What type of work environment do you prefer?** Be specific and point out some of the things you know about the environment of the company you're applying to.

_____

_____

_____

_____

_____

_____

10. **How would your boss and coworkers describe you?** Pull out strengths and traits you haven't already discussed in the interview, such as your strong work ethic or your willingness to pitch in on other projects.

_____

_____

_____

_____

_____

_____

11. **Why was there a gap in your employment?** Be direct about the reason and talk about how the experience shaped you into the person you are today. Mention any training, volunteer work, or mind-enriching activities you've done.

_____

_____
_____
_____
_____
_____
_____

12. **How do you deal with pressure or stressful situations?** Choose an answer that shows you can meet a stressful situation head-on in a productive, positive way.

_____
_____
_____
_____
_____
_____

13. **What do you like to do outside of work?** Briefly sharing is okay if you're asked about your hobbies outside of work.

_____
_____
_____
_____
_____
_____

14. **Do you have any questions for us?** If you haven't had the chance to tell your story yet, this is the ideal time to do so. Start with, "I don't have any (more) questions, but I would like to tell you something about myself…." This is the perfect opportunity to discuss the challenges you've overcome.

_____
_____
_____
_____
_____
_____

## Video 10 – Section 9. Workplace Advancement and Transferable Skills

What are your transferrable skills and how can you develop new ones in your current situation?

_____
_____
_____
_____
_____

## <u>Video 11 – Section 10. Being Part of a Team</u>

Describe a situation that shows you being a good teammate.

_____

_____

_____

_____

_____

_____

_____

## <u>Video 12 – Section 11. Workplace Conflict</u>

Describe a time you used negotiation to resolve a situation before it got out of control.

_____

_____

_____

_____

_____

_____

_____

## <u>Video 13 – Section 12. Peer Support & Summary</u>

List some advantages to accepting help from others.

_____

_____

_____

_____

_____

_____

_____

## ADDITIONAL ACTIVITIES

### Resentment

It is said that resentment is like drinking poison and waiting for the other person to die. Undoubtedly, incarceration fosters resentment. Making a deliberate choice to see where our resentments stem from and identifying how it can negatively affect our pursuit of happiness.

Make a list of three people, organizations, or situations in which you hold resentment:

1. _____
2. _____
3. _____
4. _____
5. _____

How can these resentments affect:

- Your relationships

  _____
  _____

- Your peace of mind

  _____
  _____

- Your happiness

  _____
  _____

- Your goal pursuits

  _____
  _____

### Trusted Circle

One key factor in successfully navigating both incarceration and re-entry is to identify a "Trusted Circle." Individuals who you can rely on for support, encouragement, and most of all, honesty. They are the ones that tell us if we are contemplating doing something that is not good for us. They have experience in dealing with the challenges we are confronting. Most of all they want the best for us and aren't s seeking to take advantage of us. Identify the following:

Mentors whom you respect

_____
_____
_____

Peers with shared experiences

_____
_____
_____

Trusted family members

_____
_____
_____

Professionals (therapists, case managers)

_____
_____
_____

# A PATH TO FINANCIAL FREEDOM©

## Video 1 – Introduction

What concerns do you have about financially getting back on your feet?

_____
_____
_____
_____
_____
_____
_____

## Video 2 – Section 1. Financial Goals

How do you define financial freedom?

_____
_____
_____
_____
_____
_____
_____

What are your financial goals three years after your release?

_____
_____
_____
_____
_____
_____

## Video 3 – Section 2. Banking Basics

What are some services banks provide that can benefit us financially?

_____
_____
_____
_____
_____
_____

## Video 4 – Section 3. Budgeting

Think needs vs wants.

| Budget Worksheet | Monthly Amount |
|---|---|
| **NET INCOME** | |
| Wages | |
| Support payments | |
| Other | |
| **TOTAL INCOME** | |
| | |
| **EXPENSES** | |
| **Household Expenses** | |
| Mortgage or rent | |
| Homeowners' or renters' insurance | |
| Real estate taxes | |
| Gas/Electric/Water/Sewer and Garbage | |
| Cell phone(s) | |
| Cable/Internet/streaming services | |
| Groceries, household supplies, and toiletries | |
| Other | |
| **Transportation Expenses** | |
| Car payment | |
| Vehicle repairs and maintenance | |
| Insurance, license, and city stickers | |
| Gasoline | |
| Taxi, ride-share, bus, and train | |
| Parking | |
| **Personal Expenses** | |
| Medical (out-of-pocket expenses) | |
|     Health insurance | |
|     Rx and over-the-counter medicines | |
| Clothing | |
| Laundry/dry cleaning | |
| Grooming (hair, nails, etc.) | |
| Entertainment, dining out, and hobbies | |
| Other | |
| **Payments/Debts** | |
| Child Support | |
| Credit Cards | |
| Savings Deposits | |
| | |
| **TOTAL EXPENSES** | |
| **TOTAL INCOME LESS EXPENSES** | |

## Video 5 – Section 4. Housing (Owning vs. Renting)

Compare the benefits of renting an apartment and the benefits of owning a home.

_____
_____
_____
_____
_____
_____
_____

## Video 6 – Section 5. Home Ownership

What are the advantages to the borrower in using an FHA loan to purchase a home?

_____
_____
_____
_____
_____
_____
_____

## Video 7 – Section 6. Acquiring an Automobile (Buying vs. Leasing)

What additional expenses are associated with having a car?

_____
_____
_____
_____
_____
_____
_____

Which do you think will be more advantageous for you, leasing or purchasing a vehicle? Why?

_____
_____
_____
_____
_____
_____
_____

### Video 8 – Section 7. Paying for Your Education

Do you have an interest in any education programs? Which ones?

_____

_____

_____

_____

_____

_____

_____

_____

### Video 9 – Section 8. Savings, Investments, and an Emergency Fund

What are some reasons to have an emergency fund?

_____

_____

_____

_____

_____

_____

_____

_____

### Video 10 – Section 9. Understanding Credit & Managing Your Credit Cards

How can you go about receiving a credit card?

_____

_____

_____

_____

_____

_____

_____

_____

### Video 11 – Section 10. Debt Reduction & Predatory Lending

What are some things you can do to keep credit card spending under control?

_____

_____

_____

_____

_____

_____

_____

_____

## Video 12 – Section 11. The Necessity of Insurance (Types and Function)

What are some potential consequences of driving without insurance?

_____
_____
_____
_____
_____
_____
_____
_____

## Video 13 – Section 12. Taxes, Taxes, and More Taxes

FOLD AND REMOVE

**PERSONAL AND CHECK INFORMATION**

| Emp ID: | Employee ID |
| | Employee First Name |
| | Employee Last Name |
| | Employee Street Address |
| | Employee City |
| | Employee Zipcode |
| Soc Sec #: | Social Security Number |
| Hire Date: | 01/01/2013 |
| Filing Status: | |
| Pay Period | 07/30/2013 to 08/05/2013 |
| Check Date | Pay date for Stub |
| Check #: | |
| Rout#: | routing # |
| Acc #: | account # |

**NET PAY ALLOCATIONS**

| DESCRIPTION | CURRENT($) | YTD($) |
|---|---|---|
| Net Pay: | 454.58 | 13974.50 |

**EARNINGS**

| DESCRIPTION | HRS/ UNITS | RATE | CURRENT($) | YTD ($) |
|---|---|---|---|---|
| REGULAR EARNINGS | 40 | 15.00 | 600.00 | 19200.00 |
| O/T EARNINGS (1.5) | 0 | | | |
| COMMISSIONS | | | 0.00 | 0.00 |
| PRETAX INS | | | | |
| 401K | | | 0.00 | 0.00 |
| HOURS WORKED | | | | |
| ADJUSTED GROSS EARNINGS | | | 600.00 | 19200.00 |

**DEDUCTIONS**

| DESCRIPTION | | CURRENT($) | YTD ($) |
|---|---|---|---|
| GARNISHMENTS | | 0.00 | 0.00 |
| | | 0.00 | 0.00 |
| | | 0.00 | 0.00 |
| TOTAL | | 0.00 | 0.00 |

**WITHHOLDINGS**

| DESCRIPTION | | CURRENT($) | YTD ($) |
|---|---|---|---|
| FEDERAL W/H | | 81.63 | 2612.31 |
| FICA MEDICARE | | 8.70 | 278.40 |
| FICA SOC-SEC (OASDI) | | 37.20 | 1190.40 |
| STATE W/H | | 17.88 | 572.20 |

## Video 14 – Summary

What did you learn from this course that you consider valuable as you prepare for release?

_____

_____

_____

_____

_____

_____

_____

# VALUES-ALIGNED GOAL SETTING©

## Video 1 – Introduction

What is the last goal you set for yourself?

_____
_____
_____
_____
_____
_____
_____

## Video 2 – Section 1. Setting Goals: Making a Commitment in Writing

What challenges do pursuing goals in your current environment pose?

_____
_____
_____
_____
_____
_____
_____

## Video 3 – Section 2. Life-Changing Events

What are your life-changing events and how have they changed you?

_____
_____
_____
_____
_____
_____
_____

## Video 4 – Section 3. Rules for Defining Success

Success is personal. What makes you feel successful today?

_____
_____
_____
_____

What does your personal success look like three years from today/release?

_____
_____
_____
_____
_____
_____
_____
_____

## Video 5 – Section 4. Universal Ingredients of Success

How have you taken responsibility for your situation?

_____
_____
_____
_____
_____
_____
_____
_____

## Video 6 – Section 5. Is That All There Is to It?

What makes you happy in the present?

_____
_____
_____
_____
_____
_____
_____
_____

What do you believe will make you happy in the future? (Be descriptive.)

_____
_____
_____
_____
_____
_____
_____
_____
_____
_____

## Video 7 – Section 6. Define What You Stand For

**PARTIAL LIST OF VALUES**

| | | | |
|---|---|---|---|
| Achievement | Flexible | Enthusiastic | Leader |
| Adaptability | Focused | Loving | Respected |
| Adventure | Forgiving | Loyal | Responsible |
| Affection | Friendship | Mature | Sincere |
| Alertness | Generous | Modest | Sociable |
| Ambition | Gentleness | Optimistic | Strong |
| Assertive | Good Attitude | Patient | Successful |
| Authentic | Good Humor | Happy | Talented |
| Boldness | Conscientious | Hardworking | Persistent |
| Calmness | Considerate | Helpful | Polite |
| Capable | Courage | Honest | Precise |
| Caring | Creative | Humble | Professional |
| Clear Thinking | Dependable | Independent | Resourceful |
| Compassionate | Dynamic | Integrity | Tolerant |
| Competent | Educated | Joyous | Trustworthy |
| Confident | Effective | Kind | Truthful |
| Faith | Energetic | Knowledgeable | Warm |

Identify 3-5 values you hold as most meaningful in your life and explain why.

_____
_____
_____
_____
_____
_____
_____

## Video 8 – Section 7. What Really Matters

List the initials of the five people with whom you spend the most time. Place a + or – symbol next to their initials to indicate whether they are generally a positive or negative person in your life. What does this tell you about the people with whom you associate?

_____
_____
_____
_____
_____

How can I remove negative thoughts and influences when I am in a negative environment?

_____
_____
_____
_____
_____

## Video 9 – Section 8. The Role of Hope and Optimism

How can you use goals to make you feel more positive?

_____
_____
_____
_____
_____
_____
_____

## Video 10 – Section 9. Values-Aligned Goal Setting© Definitions

Jot down your ideas about a bedrock goal and two building goals.

_____
_____
_____
_____
_____
_____
_____

## Video 11 – Part 1 Recap

Are you ready to set some goals for yourself? Are there any videos you'd like to re-watch before moving ahead?

_____
_____
_____
_____
_____
_____

## Video 12 – Section 10. Values and Goal Striving

How has your conduct in the past been more concerned about how others view you (extrinsic) or how you view yourself (intrinsic)?

_____
_____

_____
_____
_____
_____
_____
_____

## Video 13 – Section 11. Discover Your Passion

What have you been passionate about in your life? Why?

_____
_____
_____
_____
_____
_____
_____
_____

## Video 14 – Section 12. Determining Your Bedrock Goal

How can the Law of Attraction apply to you? What will make people want to be a part of your circle?

_____
_____
_____
_____
_____
_____
_____

## Video 15 – Section 13. Specific Activities

What does the phrase "Specific Activities are easy to understand but difficult to execute" mean to you?

_____
_____
_____
_____
_____
_____
_____

## Video 16 – Section 14. Obstacles

What internal obstacles and what external obstacles do you foresee as you move forward?

_____

_____
_____
_____
_____
_____
_____
_____

## Video 17 – Section 15. Resources

What resources will you need moving forward to pursue your chosen goals?

_____
_____
_____
_____
_____
_____
_____
_____

## Video 18 – Section 16. Small Victories

What small victories can you celebrate in your current environment?

_____
_____
_____
_____
_____
_____
_____

## Video 19 – Section 17. Determine Your Building Goals

What are things you want to accomplish that you can get excited about?

_____
_____
_____
_____
_____
_____
_____

It's time to put your goals and plans in writing. Fill out the following worksheet.

## Goal and Activity Development Worksheet

BEDROCK GOAL: _____

Why is this your most important goal? Are you passionate about this goal? Does it align with your stated values?

_____

_____

_____

_____

What Specific Activities support this goal and with what frequency? Are they realistic?

| What? | How Often? |
|---|---|
| _____ | _____ |
| _____ | _____ |
| _____ | _____ |

What potential obstacles might be encountered in pursuit of this goal and how will you overcome them?

| Obstacle? | Strategy? |
|---|---|
| _____ | _____ |
| _____ | _____ |
| _____ | _____ |

What resources do you need to pursue this goal and are they available?

| Resources? | Available/Substitute? |
|---|---|
| _____ | _____ |
| _____ | _____ |
| _____ | _____ |

What Small Victories will you celebrate in pursuit of this goal?

| | |
|---|---|
| _____ | _____ |
| _____ | _____ |
| _____ | _____ |

### The Joy is in the Journey

## Goal and Activity Development Worksheet

**BUILDING GOAL #1:**_____

Why is this your most important goal? Are you passionate about this goal? Does it align with your stated values?

_____

_____

_____

_____

What Specific Activities support this goal and with what frequency? Are they realistic?

| What? | How Often? |
|---|---|
| _____ | _____ |
| _____ | _____ |
| _____ | _____ |

What potential obstacles might be encountered in pursuit of this goal and how will you overcome them?

| Obstacle? | Strategy? |
|---|---|
| _____ | _____ |
| _____ | _____ |
| _____ | _____ |

What resources do you need to pursue this goal and are they available?

| Resources? | Available/Substitute? |
|---|---|
| _____ | _____ |
| _____ | _____ |
| _____ | _____ |

What Small Victories will you celebrate in pursuit of this goal?

| | |
|---|---|
| _____ | _____ |
| _____ | _____ |
| _____ | _____ |

### The Joy is in the Journey

2ND OPPORTUNITY PROGRAM PERSONAL RE-ENTRY PLAN

## Goal and Activity Development Worksheet

**BUILDING GOAL #2:** _____

Why is this your most important goal? Are you passionate about this goal? Does it align with your stated values?

_____

_____

_____

_____

What Specific Activities support this goal and with what frequency? Are they realistic?

| What? | How Often? |
|-------|------------|
| _____ | _____ |
| _____ | _____ |
| _____ | _____ |

What potential obstacles might be encountered in pursuit of this goal and how will you overcome them?

| Obstacle? | Strategy? |
|-----------|-----------|
| _____ | _____ |
| _____ | _____ |
| _____ | _____ |

What resources do you need to pursue this goal and are they available?

| Resources? | Available/Substitute? |
|------------|------------------------|
| _____ | _____ |
| _____ | _____ |
| _____ | _____ |

What Small Victories will you celebrate in pursuit of this goal?

| | |
|-------|-------|
| _____ | _____ |
| _____ | _____ |
| _____ | _____ |

**The Joy is in the Journey**

## Goal and Activity Development Worksheet

**BUILDING GOAL #3:** _____

Why is this your most important goal? Are you passionate about this goal? Does it align with your stated values?

_____

_____

_____

_____

What Specific Activities support this goal and with what frequency? Are they realistic?

| What? | How Often? |
|-------|------------|
| _____ | _____ |
| _____ | _____ |
| _____ | _____ |

What potential obstacles might be encountered in pursuit of this goal and how will you overcome them?

| Obstacle? | Strategy? |
|-----------|-----------|
| _____ | _____ |
| _____ | _____ |
| _____ | _____ |

What resources do you need to pursue this goal and are they available?

| Resources? | Available/Substitute? |
|------------|----------------------|
| _____ | _____ |
| _____ | _____ |
| _____ | _____ |

What Small Victories will you celebrate in pursuit of this goal?

| | |
|-----------|-----------|
| _____ | _____ |
| _____ | _____ |
| _____ | _____ |

**The Joy is in the Journey**

## Goal and Activity Development Worksheet

**BUILDING GOAL #4:** _____

Why is this your most important goal? Are you passionate about this goal? Does it align with your stated values?

_____

_____

_____

_____

What Specific Activities support this goal and with what frequency? Are they realistic?

| What? | How Often? |
|---|---|
| _____ | _____ |
| _____ | _____ |
| _____ | _____ |

What potential obstacles might be encountered in pursuit of this goal and how will you overcome them?

| Obstacle? | Strategy? |
|---|---|
| _____ | _____ |
| _____ | _____ |
| _____ | _____ |

What resources do you need to pursue this goal and are they available?

| Resources? | Available/Substitute? |
|---|---|
| _____ | _____ |
| _____ | _____ |
| _____ | _____ |

What Small Victories will you celebrate in pursuit of this goal?

| | |
|---|---|
| _____ | _____ |
| _____ | _____ |
| _____ | _____ |

## Video 20 – Recap

Are you satisfied with your Goal Setting Worksheets? Are there any videos you'd like to re-watch before moving ahead?

_____

_____

## Video 21 – Section 18. Making It Work

In what ways do you think you'll need to be flexible in pursuing your goals?

_____

_____

_____

_____

_____

_____

_____

## Video 22 – Section 19. Self-Discipline

How can you strengthen your self-discipline in your current situation?

_____

_____

_____

_____

_____

_____

_____

## Video 23 – Section 20. Mental Laws

How can you control your thoughts in your current environment?

_____

_____

_____

_____

_____

_____

_____

## Video 24 – Section 21. Threatening Environment/Impact Domain

How can you minimize spending your energy on things you have no control over?

_____

_____
_____
_____
_____
_____
_____
_____

## Video 25 – Section 22. Time Management: Organize & Execute Around Priorities

What are some things you can eliminate that waste your time so you can do more productive things?

_____
_____
_____
_____
_____
_____
_____
_____

## Video 26 – Section 23. Habits and Rewards: Their Role in Goal Pursuit

What are some habits you have that you'd like to change? How might you do this?

_____
_____
_____
_____
_____
_____
_____
_____

## Video 27 – Section 24. Modify the Habit Routine

What keystone habit do you wish to develop? Why?

_____
_____
_____
_____
_____
_____
_____

## Video 28 – Section 25. Recap: Goals, Happiness, and Re-Goaling

What have you done to make sure the goals you have established are things to which you are truly committed?

_____

_____
_____
_____
_____
_____
_____

## Video 29 – Section 26. Conclusion

Congratulations on completing this course. A great Small Victory. How does it feel?

_____
_____
_____
_____
_____
_____
_____
_____

## ADDITIONAL ACTIVITIES

## Rapid Fire Goals

Think of your goals in the following categories and write down the first thing that pops into your mind:

Financial Goals

_____
_____
_____

Career Goals

_____
_____
_____

Free Time Goals

_____
_____
_____

Health and Fitness Goals

_____
_____
_____

Relationship Goals

_____
_____
_____

Personal Development Goals

_____
_____
_____

## **Obstacle Worksheet**

Bedrock Goal: _____

What are some potential obstacles that will prevent you from reaching this goal? Are they Internal or External Obstacles?

- •   _____   Internal or External:_____

- •   _____   Internal or External:_____

- •   _____   Internal or External:_____

What can you change to reduce internal/self-defeating thoughts and actions that stand in the way of achieving what is important to you?

_____
_____
_____

Building Goal:_____

What are some potential obstacles that will prevent you from reaching this goal? Are they Internal or External Obstacles?

- •   _____   Internal or External:_____

- •   _____   Internal or External:_____

- •   _____   Internal or External:_____

What can you change to reduce internal/self-defeating thoughts and actions that stand in the way of achieving what is important to you?

_____
_____
_____

What are my strengths and unique traits?

_____
_____
_____

What can I do well, if I apply myself and commit the necessary efforts my strengths and unique traits?

_____
_____
_____

## **Gratitude List**

Maintaining a positive attitude is essential to survive incarceration and have a successful re-entry so we can get on with our lives. One effective activity I used is to make a daily gratitude list. I write down three things for which I am grateful. Some days this can be very challenging, other days it is obvious. Once you make this a habit, it is something you can use to start your day in a positive frame of mind.

Today I am grateful for:
1. _____
2. _____
3. _____

Today I am grateful for:
1. _____
2. _____
3. _____

Today I am grateful for:
1. _____
2. _____
3. _____

Today I am grateful for:
1. _____
2. _____
3. _____

Today I am grateful for:
1. _____
2. _____
3. _____

Today I am grateful for:
1. _____
2. _____
3. _____

Today I am grateful for:
1. _____
2. _____
3. _____

Today I am grateful for:
1. _____
2. _____
3. _____

Today I am grateful for:
1. _____
2. _____
3. _____

Today I am grateful for:
1. _____
2. _____
3. _____

Today I am grateful for:
1. _____
2. _____
3. _____

Today I am grateful for:
1. _____
2. _____
3. _____

Today I am grateful for:
1. _____
2. _____
3. _____

Today I am grateful for:
1. _____
2. _____
3. _____

Today I am grateful for:
1. _____
2. _____
3. _____

Today I am grateful for:
1. _____
2. _____
3. _____

# A PATH TO ADVANCED SKILLS©

## Video 1 – Introduction

How can an apprenticeship help you post-release?

_____

_____

_____

_____

_____

_____

_____

## Video 2 – Section 1. What are Advanced Skills?

What are three careers that interest you?

_____

_____

_____

_____

_____

_____

_____

## Video 3 – Section 2. Discover and Develop

When it comes to a future career when you _Begin with the End in Mind_ what do you see?

_____

_____

_____

_____

_____

_____

_____

## Video 4 – Section 3. Start with a Clean Slate

Have you given yourself a "clean slate?" If not, what is holding you back? _(Please recall Personal Responsibility and Self-Forgiveness from Values-Aligned Goal Setting©)_

_____

_____

_____

_____
_____
_____
_____

## Video 5 – Section 4. Being Positive and Productive

In what ways can you spend your time engaging your mind in positive thoughts?

_____
_____
_____
_____
_____
_____
_____

## Video 6 – Section 5. Proven Paths to Success

How can the Department of Labor and American Job Centers help you upon release?

_____
_____
_____
_____
_____
_____
_____

## Video 7 – Section 6. Advancing Skills on the Inside

In what way would an apprenticeship be appealing to you? Do any apprenticeship opportunities sound interesting?

_____
_____
_____
_____
_____
_____
_____

## Video 8 – Section 7. My Lived Experience

How do you think an apprenticeship can help you upon re-entry?

_____
_____

_____
_____
_____
_____
_____
_____

## Video 9 – Section 8. Completing An Apprenticeship on the Outside

What is your first step in checking into an apprenticeship program?

_____
_____
_____
_____
_____
_____
_____
_____

## Video 10 – Section 9. Benefits of an Apprenticeship

What about an apprenticeship appeals to you? What are you uncertain of?

_____
_____
_____
_____
_____
_____
_____
_____

# A PATH TO HIGHER EDUCATION©

## Video 1 – Introduction

How can higher education help you to re-enter society?

_____
_____
_____
_____
_____
_____
_____

## Video 2 – Section 1. What is Higher Education

In what ways would pursuing an education benefit you?

_____
_____
_____
_____
_____
_____
_____

## Video 3 – Section 2. Benefits of Higher Education

What would you find the greatest challenge in taking college classes?

_____
_____
_____
_____
_____
_____
_____

## Video 4 – Section 3. Challenges and Barriers

How would taking college classes bring value to you so you would be willing to deal with the challenges and barriers?

_____
_____
_____
_____
_____
_____
_____

## Video 5 – Section 4. Paying for Your Education

How does the opportunity of having higher education paid for affect your desire to enroll in an education program?

_____
_____
_____
_____
_____
_____
_____

## Video 6 – Section 5.  What Types of Programs Are Available?

What advantages do you see in taking a certificate program that requires only six courses?

_____
_____
_____
_____
_____
_____
_____

## Video 7 – Section 6.  Access to Education

How would achieving one of these degrees or certificates change your outlook on a career?

_____
_____
_____
_____
_____
_____

## Video 8 – Section 7.   My Lived Experience & Lessons Learned

How do you think taking college classes can help you upon re-entry?

_____
_____
_____
_____
_____
_____
_____

# RESUME WORKSHEET

**Contact Information**

Name: _____

Address: _____

Phone: _____

Email: _____

Objective (what type of work are you seeking?)

_____

_____

_____

_____

_____

_____

**Skill Summary**

_____

_____

_____

_____

_____

_____

**Work Experience**

Employer: _____

City & State: _____

Job Title: _____

Dates: _____

Job Responsibilities:

_____

_____

_____

_____

Employer: _____

City & State: _____

Job Title: _____

Dates: _____

Job Responsibilities:

_____

_____

_____

Employer: _____

City & State: _____

Job Title: _____

Dates: _____

Job Responsibilities:

_____

_____

_____

_____

Employer: _____

City & State: _____

Job Title: _____

Dates: _____

Job Responsibilities:

_____

_____

_____

_____

**Education**

School: _____

City & State: _____

Dates: _____

Program/Degree, Diploma, or Certificate: _____

_____

School: _____

City & State: _____

Dates: _____

Program/Degree, Diploma, or Certificate: _____

_____

School: _____

City & State: _____

Dates: _____

Program/Degree, Diploma, or Certificate: _____

_____

Use additional sheets of paper if necessary.

# RE-ENTRY CHECKLIST

**Pre-Release:**

❑ Get your medical records

❑ Confirm your housing

❑ Obtain proof of any education or classes you completed while incarcerated

❑ Ask family or friends to bring you some necessities on the day of your release

❑ Begin your job search

**Post-Release:**

❑ Have your identification documents in order

❑ Find out about outstanding fines, fees, debts, or warrants

❑ If you are a veteran, make sure you have your military discharge papers

❑ Get a working phone/phone number

❑ Find somewhere to access the internet (public libraries are plentiful and free)

❑ Create an email address

❑ Signup for health insurance

❑ Get proof of your GED/High School diploma

❑ Confirm your selective service status

❑ Open a bank account

❑ Get legal assistance if you need it

❑ Focus on rebuilding relationships

**Both Pre- and Post-Release:**

❑ Don't forget to take care of yourself

❑ Continue your education

❑ Connect with assistance programs and community organizations that can help

# Congratulations on Completing the Program!

## Contact Us

We're always happy to hear from you and to help however we can.
Here's how you and your family members can reach us:

**2nd Opportunity L3C * 2nd Opp Media Group LLC**

**Website:** 2ndopp.com

**Email:** reentry@2ndopp.com

*Be sure to visit our website (or have your friends or family sign up) to get the latest news, updates, and useful content.*

# ABOUT THE AUTHOR

**Augie Ghilarducci** knows what it's like to be at a crossroads and to need a second opportunity. After owning and operating a financial planning firm for fourteen years, he made a series of bad decisions that led to him being convicted of white-collar crimes. He served 13 years in Federal Prison before returning to Chicago in July 2017. He presently resides in Atlanta.

To make sense of his experience, Augie used his time in prison to help others. He spoke about his ethical failures at high schools, colleges, and businesses for almost a decade as part of a community outreach program. He also developed a series of employment readiness, financial literacy, life skills, and barriers to re-entry courses that he taught to fellow inmates. When he was released, he turned his passion into a second career empowering those dealing with incarceration, addiction, trauma, loss, and other life-changing events to break the chains of the past and create a positive new future. He has written essays *A Parallel Path, Collaboration for Social Benefit, It Takes More than a Job, and It Begins in Jail*™.

Augie draws on his lived experience to speak both in person and virtually in jails and prisons, substance abuse recovery centers, drug courts, halfway houses, probation departments, juvenile detention centers, and diversion programs. The message provides a practical approach to raising awareness as to how individuals can find and stay on the right path, and to law enforcement about making inmates more productive to help make jails safer.

Augie was featured in a recent *American Jails* Magazine article and spoke at the 2023 Correctional Education Association (CEA) Leadership Conference, Indiana Criminal Justice Association (ICJA), Louisiana Corrections Association (LCA), and Arkansas Jail Resources Conference. He has achieved a Master's Certificate in Business Ethics and an MBA since being released in 2017, having started both while incarcerated. Augie now shares the 2nd Opportunity Program in jails, prisons, and post-release agencies around the country.

Made in the USA
Columbia, SC
06 January 2025

48794982R00026